**Letters
to
Five Artists**

Letters
to
Five Artists

Poems by John Wain

Macmillan

© *John Wain* 1969

First published 1969 by
MACMILLAN AND CO LTD
Little Essex Street London W C 2
and also at Bombay Calcutta and Madras
Macmillan South Africa (Publishers) Pty Ltd
Johannesburg
The Macmillan Company of Australia Pty Ltd Melbourne
The Macmillan Company of Canada Ltd Toronto
Gill and Macmillan Ltd Dublin

Printed in Great Britain by
NORTHUMBERLAND PRESS LIMITED
Gateshead

DEDICATION

The individual 'letters' are, of course, dedicated to those to whom they are addressed. The collection as a whole, inasmuch as the wholeness binds them into a unity and calls something distinct into being, is offered, in humility, to the ghost of Django Reinhardt.

ACKNOWLEDGMENTS

The author gratefully acknowledges financial help from the Arts Council of Great Britain in 1969/70.

'Junk Sculptures' has appeared in *The Malahat Review* (Victoria, British Columbia); 'Music on the Water' in that review and also in *Tracks* (University of Warwick); 'Moondust' in *The Poetry Review* and also in *Frontiers of Going*, an anthology of 'space poems' published by Panther Books Ltd; 'Green Fingers' in *The Critical Quarterly* and also in *Best Poems of 1967* (Borestone Mountain Poetry Awards, 20th Annual Volume), Palo Alto, California: Pacific Books.

A NOTE

Except for the Introductory Poem, which is put there as an archway through which the rest can be approached in the right perspective, all these poems are intended to stand by themselves; but also to take on another dimension when read together and seen as one larger work. Hence certain key-figures (Ovid, Villon) crop up at several points in the volume.

I have not hesitated to blend material entirely personal to me (friendships, personal associations, tendrils of a *pietas* for place and family) with material that is 'general' and out in the open. This is because I can never see human life except as an inextricable scrambling of private and public. My imagination is alerted by history—by the different routes that men, and races of men, must travel so as to arrive at what seems, to everyone but themselves, the same point in time and space. Every individual foreground has a racial and national background. In this respect the present volume carries further a theme already dominant in an earlier long poem of mine, *Wildtrack*, with its inward-looking Night-self and outward-looking Day-self that together constitute the human personality.

An artist is a particularly suitable focus for this kind of meditation. When we make a friend of an artist, those personal qualities that evoke our love and admiration are intimately related to the qualities of the work, the public statement that he or she has given to the world. When I think of the artists who are my friends, my thoughts inevitably move on two levels, and so perhaps have a chance of reflecting some of the complex truth about man and his situation.

Finally I will add, for the benefit of critics who might otherwise have to do a great deal of counting on their fingers, that the rhythm of these poems, while allowing of frequent departure and return, is basically the deca-syllable or 'iambic pentameter'. This is the metre of English poetry when English poetry is in serious vein, and recent attempts to find a substitute for it have given me the impression—to take over a phrase of George Orwell's—of 'fleas hopping amid the ruins of a civilisation'.

J.W.
Oxford and Vincennes, 1969

Introductory Poem addressed to all the friends to whom these Poems are written: About Exile, and a Roman Poet on a Ship, and a Modern Poet at an Airport, and Red Indians, and Horsemen on the Ice, and a Boy in 1900

THE salt wind carries no land-smells. Even
the birds have gone back. Indifferent, they
scream on the cliffs, watch for the next boat
setting out.
                    Now the world is water.
Soil must have fed these timbers long ago,
when I had no name. Now those packed grains
root-sheltering, calm, warmed with Italian sun
are a memory. Their world, like mine, is the waves
the bearded rocks far under the waves, and the monsters
our minds cannot guess at, waiting there.

Even my mind?

                    So fed with prodigies,
instructed in the suddenness of change,
beast's head, arms of a shrub? A girl's
smooth-running limbs turned to a sliding stream?

Even now, cast out, shamed, it is the same mind,
made nimble by leaping among prodigies:

I, if anyone, could name the unnamed who swim

mindlessly waiting in their salty gloom?
No. I fear them too much. Water changes all.

I, lover of women, those swelling gourds,
I devotee of liquefaction: shape
dissolved in shape, stiff blood-crammed pleasure
dissolved in warmth and wetness: I, the singer
of change and melting, the lazy river
of pleasure winding through the seasons,
the girls new-named, new-faced, but always the same girl:
I, now, to learn about water!
      To hear the creak
of the strained ropes, the loud complaint
of timbers sawn from their green and changing trees,
planed, caulked, sent floating far from the smell of land:

to lie on this wooden bunk, lonely and sick
and hear the merciless waves drum on the hull
telling me:
    this, after all, is the nature of water!

The baby floats in a living pond:
      The grown man
thirsts for the eager juice of a ripe girl.
wetness, wetness!
     fountains in the dusty squares,
the quick live jet that danced in the dry air,
the splash and cool drip over the stone lip,
like love, like easy love:
Haunches and breasts like ripe halves of a peach!
Now water prods and slaps me purple. Deep
in its belly the empty-eyed
monsters hide.
    Was this always
true? Did water breed monsters, predatory

teeth honed for a poet's flesh,
from the beginning?
Ars Amatoria. That thirst undid me.
I changed. I wrote of change. Of how
life danced, and danced, and never would be still.
This, too, was thirst: was thirst for the same drink,
for heat and liquid change liquid and heat,
men alter girls, girls change the lives of men:

but still the dusty throat
cried thirst, and only thirst, chewed my dry lines
and drank the salty juice, and cried more thirst,

and after nine years the unreachable man
with a god's mask, took from a slave's hand
his golden stylus and wrote down my name,
snapped shut the blazing jewel-case of Rome
with me outside, crying, for ever outside.

Liquid, liquid undid me.
                          Washed, floated
away out of memory. Soft girls
trapped my thoughts hard. These waves
can beat timber to a pulp.
                        To learn about water . . .

Publius Ovidius Naso, this is you!

You, and not only you. The poet's flesh
is always divided and swallowed among whispers.
Whisper of grain on grain, of undersea
siftings, of ritual enacted without passion,
enacted so that the channel shall stay open
to belief, to passion, to the trembling FIAT.

You, Ovidius, and not only you, are exiled.

BOAC announce the departure of their flight
whateveritis
will passengers for this flight please
go to the top of the main staircase

See him rise from his nervous seat
flight-bag and magazines clutched in his hand
stomach already soothed with Dramamine
Dogrose, the poet in a drip-dry
suit, on his way to an
INTERNATIONAL CULTURAL CONFERENCE (fare paid,
hotel arranged: now, Dogrose, you're
an established poet who gets asked to conferences.
friend, go up higher:
Go to the top of the main staircase!)

Adriatic waves thump the hull. The big jets
scream like trapped gulls out on the tarmac.
Gales of the sea trapped permanently in metal.
Dogrose, neat-suited, Dramamined, a true
poet with his sea-water blood
pumping through valves of indolence and lust,
shy, watchful, quick to detect a slight,
haunted by rhythms of indifferent drums,
stung out of lethargy by images
which touch his flesh like loved fingers, he rises,
this poet, and obeys the metal speaker:

go to the top of the main staircase
go to the top of the main staircase

wave after wave of voyagers, outwardly
calm with discipline and information,
inwardly shrilling like electric bells

(who am I? what will become of me? WHERE
IS HOME? are they going to kill me?)

go to the top of the main staircase

the exact procedure of a slaughterhouse!
The herd, horns clicking, eyes rolling in fear,
bawling and fouling the neat passageway,
go to the top of the main staircase where
their necks are automatically, neatly, broken.

So Dogrose on his way to represent
poetry, the controlling agony, the creative
agony in the formal garden, goes
with the herd, to the top of the main staircase.

Relegatio. Technically the milder of the two Roman forms
of banishment. The other, *exsilium*, involved loss of citizenship and confiscation of property, but at least the *exsul*
was free to wander the whole earth save within a prescribed radius from the city of Rome. Tomis (modern
Kustenje) was obviously chosen as a place Ovid would
hate.

Relegatio to Kustenje: the cold salt wind,
treeless and marshbound, on a rocky coast,
scene of an always-renewed humiliation:
this was Ovid's luck.
                    And Dogrose's?

oh, *exsilium*: he can go anywhere,
blown along like a leaf, he can go anywhere,
like a scrap of orange peel on the restless water,
he can go anywhere,

except to the city.

Dogrose, you long for the city,

                              the city of art,

the ranged towers of fulfilment, the squares of thought,
the city where all cool poetry is true,
where morning haze melts and everything is seen,
but not wearily, not with hot sanded eyes,
because everything is seen to be in motion,
the motion of a dance, a perpetual arrival:
Dogrose, Dogrose, you have dreamed of this city,
but never entered it or heard its murmur,
except sometimes in sleep, or in your art,
when your art happened to be honest and fortunate.

So, Dogrose, your sentence is *exsilium*.

Ovid at least knew the city he longed for:
pacing the cobbles of Tomis, gazing out
with fear and loathing at the frozen marshes,
he could have drawn you, on the spot, a plan
of the city he loved, told you in detail
what everyone was doing at that moment.

stone,
golden stone
warmth-retaining golden stone
sun-quickened warmth-retaining golden stone
noon-polished sun-quickened warmth-retaining golden
   stone

stairs
cool stairs

   18

seen-through-doorways cool stairs
eye-resting seen-through-doorways cool stairs
impudent eye-resting seen-through-doorways cool stairs

girl
shadowy girl
warmth-retaining shadowy girl
impudent warmth-retaining shadowy girl
seen-through-doorway warmth-retaining shadowy girl

on the sensual stairs

                    noon-polished

bright as the coins that buy her
clinking in my palm

after the wine and the good talk
the hearing of verses.

Yes, I remember the city
and the city's joys
and its golden stones

and I look out across these stiff salt grasses

Relegatio from the known, identified place:
or *exsilium* in a world of aching gaps,
of spaces where possibility might be, where
voyaging hope might find anything or nothing:

take your choice, and in either case,
and even if you have no choice at all,
go to the top of the main staircase!

Now the deep Danube
is damned. Winter in the locked heart
of the poet, snow on the salt marshes:
millions of flakes falling on the endless Atlantic,
and on that other Atlantic of grass,
cruised by mammal ships.

To the west
of the western landfall. Men know it only
by report. The grass
goes on for ever, and the dark-humped herds
no one can count.

Ice tinkles in their coats
now, the same ice that rimes the heart of Ovid.
(*Whither, unto the bed's foot, life is shrunk*)
The Northern hemisphere endures, endures.
The red man makes a fire of buffalo dung
on the treeless plain (Lee Lubbers, are you there?
The Redskin also has his treasure amid
the unregarded, the carelessly dropped waste).

The great herds move. And with them move the men,
the women, and the children, and the tents.

But progress came
the iron ships came
the railroads came
the automatic rifle with
telescopic sights, came

If innocence exists
we see it in that eye
that patient, shaggy head
but innocence is air
through which the bullet flies
through which the axe-blade falls

As it fell on the Jews
as it fell on the gipsies
innocent, the children
bewildered as bison calves
herded into the camps:

Django, pluck your strings
for the gipsies who were gassed
and the gipsies now in England
herded from their camps
legislated into despair
in England now: pluck, pluck
the taut strings of our hearts.

And Bill
will listen a while, and lift
his belled horn to his lips.
The buffalo went
the Indian went
(to zoos, in either case,
when they happened to survive)

Well, now it is all over
and the plains have dwindled
to a geographical expression
a certain colour on the map, no more,

I go sometimes to the zoo
to question the buffalo
who never replies

I bend over the railings
as he stands in his pen:
colossal head and round
dark eye remembering what?

Look at a buffalo's eyes
some time. Wide-set, reflecting, round,
the boss of a polished shield

But nothing shielded him.

Francis Parkman in *The Oregon Trail* (1847) describes
the life at Fort Laramie, at that time a trading station
entirely administered by the American Fur Company, the
nearest outposts of the United States Army being seven
hundred miles to the east.

The permanent inhabitants of the fort were Indian
employees, with a few white supervisors, but it was the
rallying-point for Indian tribes on the surrounding plains
and a stopping-place for every party of emigrants on their
way to Oregon and California. The Dakota Indians, who
at that time still felt themselves stronger than the whites,
would get wind of the arrival of a wagon-train of emi-
grants at Fort Laramie, and a whole village would present
themselves and demand a 'feast'—a cup of coffee and two
or three biscuits. Parkman gives an eye-witness account of
the arrival of 'Smoke's village' at the same time as that
of a wagon-train, and of how Smoke and his people set up
their tents on the plain behind the fort, so that a whole
Indian village, loud with dogs and children, was sud-
denly there as if it had arisen from the bare earth.

'One evening about sunset the village was deserted. We
met old men, warriors, squaws, and children in gay attire,
trooping off to the encampment with faces of anticipa-
tion; and, arriving here, they seated themselves in a semi-
circle. Smoke occupied the centre, with his warriors on
either hand; the young men and boys came next, and the
squaws and children formed the horns of the crescent.
The biscuits and coffee were promptly despatched, the
emigrants staring open-mouthed at their savage guests.'

Parkman goes on:

'The Ogillallah, the Brute, and the other western bands
of the Dakota and Sioux, are thorough savages, un-
changed by any contact with civilization. Not one of them
can speak a European tongue, or has ever visited an
American settlement. Until within a year or two, when
the emigrants began to pass through their country on the
way to Oregon, they had seen no whites, except the few
employed about the Fur Company's posts. They thought
them a wise people, inferior only to themselves, living in
leather lodges, like their own, and subsisting on buffalo.
But when the swarm of *Meneaska*, with their oxen and
wagons, began to invade them, their astonishment was
unbounded. They could scarcely believe that the earth
contained such a multitude of white men. Their wonder
is now giving way to indignation; and the result, unless
vigilantly guarded against, may be lamentable in the
extreme.'

Well, what's the latest tall story
about the weather?
                              The *weather*?
Yes, that's all they talk of out here.

'Back home, they don't know what extremes
of temperature are. The other day I threw
a snowball at a man: by the time it reached him
he wasn't hit by a *snow*ball, no sir;
he was scalded by boiling water.'

The weather acts directly on our lives,
because our lives are naked. No city clothes us.
No *civitas*, no civilization. Dust
whirls on the dry wind and settles
in the hinges of our lives.
                              Weather, and war!

23

Ovid got to Kustenje in the summer.
The cobbles sweated. The salt wind
scrubbed the squares with dry heat.
What kind of place is this?

                              Salt marshes,
rocks. Above, Odessa: below, Istanbul,
behind, Bucharest.

                              Half-breed Greeks,
full-blooded barbarians. Shy eyes watching:
'This is the wicked poet sent from Rome,
to live here as a penance.'

                              'A penance? Here?
He'll soon get used to it, if he's a man.'

Unnerved. A few questions. Is this my house?
Are there any books in Latin? Does anyone
speak it, I mean correctly, like a Roman?
Do I sleep on this? Where is my servant?

A fat woman, broad-cheeked, her face secret,
speaking Samatian only.

                              She wipes her hands
ceaselessly on a coarse apron. Her husband
sweeps the courtyard. New shutters will be needed
against the winter.

                              The winter? When will that be?
Not long now. The Danube freezes
for three months. That's when they come.

When who come?

                              That's when they come,

in the winter.

They come,

they come,
galloping, bows bent.

WHO COME?

Who? What does it matter who?
The ones who always come, to any outpost:
the pitiless fierce riders from out there.

Watch that weather, stranger. When you wake
to find the water in your pitcher frozen,
then one day, soon, you'll hear the drumming hoofs.

That's why we talk so much about the weather.
And why I, too, think of the weather in 1900.
That boy's starved feet cat-quick on the hot bricks.

Burning arrows in the thatch? He makes a home
here?
His hunger makes a home.

Yes, and those streets
in 1900, a boy of six years
walking those streets, thin, his clothes
of the cheapest, nearly worn out
before he got them: but hot
incitingly hot, under his feet, the brick
pavement, for some reason I always imagine
him in summer, narrow feet
on the hot bricks.

Polluted water
and a towpath with rank

nettles and grass: the thin boy
prowls amid jagged tins. Heat
glares from the blue sky. For some
reason I see him under that hard
blue sky always, smelling polluted
water, watching the smoke
trail its thick arms across, black on blue,
and the bricks hot.

Ah, because
it is my own childhood gives me
my vision of his, the streets were the same
after three decades, the same bricks
held the same heat:

I wandered,
more often in summer than winter,
smelt the canal, was hungry like him,
I mean like him in his inner hunger, I longed
to reach out, to live, beyond these hot
bricks and round black kilns. Home!
I never doubted it, my home was hunger,
that hunger my blood had caught
from his hasty blood.

I see 1900,

trouble in South Africa, volunteers
marching with silver bands down London Road:
I see the thin boy
hungry
always hungry
for food, for life, for the promise that rises
to his narrow feet from the hot bricks.
Where does the canal go? Who reads the signal
poured across the sky by the fat kilns?
Power, money, and trouble:
Wedgwood and Kruger, Spode

and Smuts.
                The old queen
turns in her bed and dies. The thin boy,
my father, sees his mother draw the blinds.

The blinds of home. The bailiff has the chairs.
The old queen dies. Grandmother draws the blinds
on the bare dusty room. End of a world.
The kilns go belching on, and Wedgwood is
A liberal M.P.
                The boy is hungry:
He needs so many kinds of nourishment.
His hunger came to me. I have it still.

Home, home! The narrow houses and the kilns,
The stinking water. The tip above the roofs.
And half a dozen brick town halls.

Why is it always summer in my dream?

Because of the hot sunlight in his eyes?

To speak of exile is to speak of home.
The drumming hoofs across the ice: the poet
listless, far from Rome. Seventy years ago
the smell of the canal and the fat kilns.
The burning arrows crackle in the thatch.
The lost plank floats in the scum-laden water.
The poet shivers. The thin boy dreams of life.

And we speak of home? Of leaving, and returning?
A shake of the dice-box. A cube of time
rolls.

Ovid in Smoke's village. The feathered men
stare at the poet who wrote of one girl
turned to a river, another holding up
arms suddenly twigs and leaves. The plank
in the crushed weeds, inert in that canal,
reared up, hardened to stone, became a dolmen.

Dogrose, *miglior fabbro*, do up your belt:
the muzak ceases and the engines scream.
Back in the airport you were nowhere. Now
on the tarmac, soon at twelve thousand feet,
then at another airport, a bus, an hotel room,
the table and ashtrays of the conference,
still nowhere, always nowhere, and you ask
so piteously, *What am I to do?*

Why, Dogrose, plant a grove of cardboard trees
and walk beneath them in a nylon toga!
the raised plank is
dolmen and totem. Feathered men
file swiftly along the nettled towpath.
Smoke's village pitches camp at Stoke-on-Trent,
smoke's other village.

Dogrose, you seek a theme?

Still want to think and feel yourself a poet?
The dice of time is shaken, rolls and stops.
The Indians and the buffaloes are gone.
Kustenje has no poets, only Agitprop.
Pasternak appealed to Khrushchev against exile:
his Art of Love was more profound than Ovid's.
After his death, they jailed the one he loved.
The quick thin feet of that boy six years old
have passed across the stones, my friends:
have passed, and will pass, and are passing now.
And Dogrose climbs the international sky.

Music on the Water

to Bill Coleman
in Paris

                 and like
the river's slow insistence.

In winter, a great padlock. Tugs and strings of barges
fist-gripped. Summer, a cool flowing.
The sun hatches the shy turtle's eggs.

Sound moves across water:
axe-chop, bow-twang: did the Indians
sing? Or was silence their music?

The river orchestrates silence. It pours.
They looked at it and they said: *Mississippi*.

So time passed, without punctuation.
The river poured and grass waved
in the dateless wind. Red-skinned, high cheekboned Adam
named the animals: *oppossum, chipmunk*.

And sound reached out across water.

But out at sea, the corpses smacked down
into the waves, unweighted. White bodies were cheap:
still, a white sailor who died, at least

got cannon-shot at feet and head.
Sick, terrified black bodies
only just worth the cost of carrying
were chucked out if found to be dead
(putrid, not understanding, sick for Africa)
chucked out, like peelings from the galley
to float on the surface till the sharks came up.

Out at sea, the slave ships were coming.

Sound reached out across water:
dead-smack of corpse, gull-scream,
chop of the settler's axe, gun-crack and
whip-crack: in the steamy fields
the black backs bend, the long dark song goes up:
the American earth, no longer Eden:
and sound moves out across water.

Africa forgotten,
the hunter's green and yellow beads forgotten,
the snapping apart of the full bean-pod,
the stew simmered with thick yam-flour, forgotten.
The elephant's praisename is Laaye, signifying
'O death, please stop following me':
they forgot the elephant's village-shaking tread
but death did not stop following them.

Voodoo forgotten,
the necklace of teeth forgotten
and the witch-women in coastal areas
with skirts made from octopus tentacles
forgotten also

but the tentacles of misery, the tread
of death broad as the foot of Laaye:
these, they had no occasion to forget.

The Indians were gone
taking with them their music of silence:
now the black backs bent low, and the long dark song
moved out across the water:

sound of steamboat, of hammer and saw,
of locomotives, of clopping horses
and of the song of sorrowful memory,
the sound of unknown Africa.

And the cobbles of Europe
were already old:
                    the steep roofs
had kept out many seasons already

the iron cooking-pots of humble men
fed life, humble and recurrent life
stirred by women who bent and dreamed
lay down, rose up and dreamed:

                    down the slow lanes
the painted wheels were turning, dark-eyed women
crooning old foreign words to their shawled babies

words already old, the language of somewhere forgotten,
the creak of axles, their home the roadsides of Europe:

En mon pais suis en terre loingtaine

never at home, therefore always at home,
contained,
                    unspillable:
these were Django's people.
                    What centuries unwound,
what wars, what exiles, what thunder of surf,

cry of the new-born to the creak of axles,
what bruising of continent against continent,
before the two homeless songs made this their home:
the plucked string and the quivering mettlesome cry,
the two long journeys meeting here at last.

and Paris in the spring, the cold-eyed spring
hard buds, hard stones
Paris
the cold inexhaustible mother
feeding desire with hard nipples

spring:

time of the dispossessed, the voyagers,
envious only of solitude.

Sweet mother who leaves us all stranded
sweet mother who fuels our veins with hate

under whose bridges we crawl
in the rainy night
amorous as sparrows

the dark flowing Seine
inundating our nerve-centres

And Bill this is your second river
channel of paradoxes
ancient passageway of opposites.

Le sein is a masculine word:
a woman's breasts, masculine! what a race!
crazy inverted logic everywhere!
le sein is masculine, this is *la seine*,

the drag-net, the bulging tow, the trawl
that disdains nothing, the swag-belly,
full of mussels and contraceptives,
avid of mud, cress and semen,
la Seine, magnet of weightless suicides,
despair of anglers.

The first day, too inert to look for work, I borrowed a
rod and went fishing in the Seine, baiting with blue-
bottles. I hoped to catch enough for a meal, but of course
I did not. The Seine is full of dace, but they grew cunning
during the siege of Paris, and none of them has been
caught since, except in nets.
    —George Orwell, *Down and Out in Paris and London.*

A different river, Bill. But the same need.
Something human to make the cold ripples dance.
Something human out of the bell of your horn.

Aching Paris
those spring evenings in big ugly cafés
staring through plate glass at the clicking street
still unaccountably light at eight o'clock
millions of cigarettes fuming like rockets
the girls with alarm clocks ticking between their legs
the pavement sprouting dreams of Martinique

aching Paris, never resting
inexhaustible mother and ticking meretrix
timed so as to wake us in mid-orgasm
old twisted Paris, gaunt zoo of the poor,
circus ring where the sawdust is milled bone:

Et nous, les os, devenons cendre et pouldre.
De nostre mal personne ne s'en rie;
Mais priez Dieu que tous nous veuille absouldre!

Bill, it is you and only you she needs.
lip those notes! press down those cunning valves!

A thousand years have cropped that sated womb.
Ten centuries of eyesight have blanched the air.
Feet have scrubbed the stones down to dead rubble.

Even the Seine catches nothing but old string.
The European impulse has dried up.
Every seventy years a new lyricism:

She was miraculous! yes, yes, we admit it!
But now, the song-bag is finally sighed out:
different trade-winds are blowing.

Old icy cobbled Paris, twisted streets,
fifteenth century, before the slavers got going,
surf booming innocently on the African beaches
and the university of Paris already two hundred years old:
one of its graduates, bleeding from the face,
well known in that precinct, François Villon,
stumbles into the barber's shop, dropping blood.
'Friend, patch me up, I'm leaving.' 'Fighting again?'
His lip is gashed wide open. 'An insolent priest.
I sent him to the other world.'
The barber whistles, dabbing at the wound:
'That'll mean trouble with the authorities.'

François de Montcorbier, *alias* des Loges, *alias* Villon,
(*En mon pais suis en terre loingtaine*)
never from that time a stranger to trouble,
his neck never far from the hempen knot.

Freres humains qui apres nous vivez.

N'ayez les cuers contre nous endurcis

O death, please stop following me

Car, se pitie de nous povres avez,
Dieu en aura plus tost de vous mercis

O death, please stop following me
O death, please stop following me

And each continent sang its pure music.

Villon, fugitive, cudgelled, his bones cold,
laughing and singing his crystalline despair,
uttered the pure music of Europe

Je meurs de seuf aupres de la fontaine,
Chault comme feu, et tremble dent a dent;
En mon pais suis en terre loingtaine;

and under a copper sun
the pure music of Africa rose up:

flight of the egret in words:
repose of the bright parrot among leaves,
lidded pots of clay, woven shields,
quick strut of a disappearing bushfowl:
these things in words:
    song, drum and chorus.

The bright feathers fade from the mind,
the hunter's mask, the dance,
feast after hunting, contentment among straw huts,
these fade from the mind:
images pasted over with fear,
fear of the whip, fear of the chain,

of the waves, of the sea-monsters,
of the tossing prison reeking with death:
then forgotten below this, the images,
buried in marrow and blood.

And they also journeyed
the black-eyed people from the forgotten country
painted Romany wheels strained through Europe's mud

from threat to threat
cursed, harried, their caravans
fired by the soldiery, and the villages
full of hostile eyes at shutters.

From threat to threat they went,
his people, and your people.

And the long journey met at last in Paris:
met, and flowed into music.
Paris, 1935:
the neon lights shone bright
on the dark river
and the epaulettes shone bright
on the shoulders of Hitler's generals
as they bent over maps
their criss-cross sights already on Paris
they thirsted for her
the Rhine was mad to flow into the Seine
to die of joy in her grab-net
as a man wants to drive his teeth
into the white shoulders of a girl
those monocled men spread out maps
Paris, Paris, white shoulders
and behind them, the ovens
already going up
Herrenvolk

must not be jostled in the world's avenues
so build the ovens
Joe Louis knocked out Schmelling
so build the ovens
and build a special one for him.

And in neon Paris, Django strummed
his plangent greeting-chords to life
and your horn was at your lips
and sound moved out, Bill, across the water:
flow, Seine, flow, Mississippi,
flow, strangling Rhine!

Et nous, les os, devenons cendre et pouldre

And I, in by-passed England, rain on the window,
spin your records and groove down the centuries
hearing the creak of axles and the crack of whips
the murmur of women to their shawled babies.

The deep lanes of Europe: the sharks rising
to the unchained corpses: the uncatchable carp
in the *rusée* Seine, knowing all men's tricks:
knowing men to their depths, in the agony
of unillusion, as the whores
know them in the tall, scented houses,
as slaves in their patience know them
unbuttoned, unmasked, yet hung about with dreams
like mad vines swaying in the tropic night
huge flowers that when we touch them turn to scabs.

Bill, my friend, courteous and smiling,
my tall unruffled uncle, at ease in restaurants,
king of the world of easy handshakes,
anchored to Swiss Lily like a bronze statue
on a marble plinth, you know all this:

you and the gipsy Django sang it all.

And now that he is dead, you sing it still.
The night stirs the dark vines, the enslaved eyes
stare on the naked face of pitiable huge Man,

and sound, always your sound, moves out across the water.

Moondust

*for Victor Neep
in Rhosgadfan*

STONE, torrent, and the moon: broken machines.
You light your world from a dark sky. In sleep
flesh cools from the hot fevers of the day,
the mind grows calm after the waking dream
of action, choice and movement. Motionless
the mountains face the moon. Only the air
pure, silent, thinning into nothingness,
spreads its cool gulf of emptiness between them,
adding no word to their ancient dialogue
of shape and light, nothing but shape and light.

A bedstead rusting on the mountainside:
the humped stones of a wall, the inaudible
footfall of mineral ghosts: all these
exist beyond change and beyond questioning.

Is it that they died into a stronger life
beyond the life of conundrums, or did they live
always in that hard dimension of calm:

where shape and light become pure character?

old mangles
old gas cookers, limbs

of bicycles that died of old age
rest by the shifting sea, or on the mountain
content and motionless
bathed in that light
content to have arrived:
content to be, what all those wheeling years
they were becoming:
sentinels of time and loneliness,
emblems of all that is unreachable

Because she asks no questions, because her face
Holds light and only light, calm-spreading, free
Of all those interrogatives that hold us
Hot-tempered captives when the sun climbs high:
Because she is a disc of visual silence
Dramatic only in her suddenness
When breaking from the clouds, she throws her silver
On grass, on waves that rake the waves of shingle,
On rock and waterfall and moving sheep
So that all objects cast contented shadows,
Not like the shadows of day, not question marks
Crossing each gesture with a grimace of doubt.
The moon's shadows are of darkness only,
fulfilled, contained, an experience of shape.

She holds our violence in a steady frame
burnished amid pure darkness. At Stonehenge,
the victim died when dawn lit up the sky,
splashing the stone with fire that sang, *Destroy*.

MAXIMS

1. Both art and life are strongest where there is an equi-
librium of opposites, a balanced outward pull of contra-
dictions creating a strong knot at the centre.

2. The artist thrives on disadvantages. He attains wisdom because he accepts ignorance and folly. Joy comes to him often because he pitches his tent in the shadow of despair.

3. The withered hermit with his riotous dreams explores every haunt of sensuality without moving from his cell. Similarly, in every debauchee there is an anchorite, sitting motionless among the rocks.

4. It does not follow from this that sensuality and ignorance in themselves are productive. Apes are amiable creatures, but they never say anything worth writing down.

5. Reformed thieves make excellent detectives; born thieves who have never stolen anything, even better ones: that is, law is upheld by the appetite for villainy.

6. Truth is fortuitous, but a good lie takes account of the probabilities.

I clang the gate, and walk up by the wall.
Hard, stalky nettles grow beside the stones.
'There's too much cover down there,' you once said,
with a grin, speaking of broad-leaved Sussex
full of sap-smelling ditches and tall grass.
Here, the nettles grip the rained-on slope
like obstinate small pines. There are no docks.

Your house is long and low. Down on all fours,
it waits for the wind to start shooting. Bald
mountains stand round. Despair of ambushers,
the hard green hillside looms behind your roof.

Safety in exposure:

truth sitting naked on the naked rocks.
That part of you that's capable of fear
makes you stand up unsheltered on these slopes
soaking up air and starlight like a dolmen.

Everything needs its opposite.
Nothing by itself is strong enough:
not even love, not even bread.

Yet some there are who know nothing of contrarieties.
They approach knowledge frontally, like a dog lunging
for a lump of meat which he sees reflected in the water.
When temperaments like these are overcome by lust for
knowledge of the moon, they launch a
                    M O O N P R O B E

Controlled by whispering frequencies
the mindless rocket shoots and lands
in spray of dust that never leapt
till now, but sifted in a breeze
more gentle than a lover's hands.
the mindless feelers are adept.

I see the picture radio'd.
It shows a grab that fumbles out
to take a scoop of the moon's crust.
Now homeward, with your stolen load!
The rocket lifts its frozen snout.
Knowledge! the manna of the just!

I do not grudge them their delight.
The earth desires what the moon hides.
But moonlight on a woman's face
seen among silent leaves at night—
this is the power that pulls our tides.

What if we fall from the moon's grace?

Moon-knowledge. Her secret language draws the waves
into their saraband, and fertile wombs
pay her their rhythmic homage. See how these men
empty their phial of moon-dust on a sterile
dissecting-tray, and, masked, hang over it
with greedy eyes. Moon-secrets, Vic! To know
what rivers rustle in her arteries,
to name the minerals in her marrow-bones!

A prize beyond the dreams of kidnappers:
Everyone's kingdom for a vase of moon-dust!

All falsehood, greed, and foolishness. Yet we
forgive them. Eyes the moon has shone into

can never feed the brain with sanity.
Always a trace of madness filters through.

Their measurements and probes, your reverie,
are both moon-drenched, yet you know that you do

only what must be done, or life would be
entwined, embraced, and crushed by death. So few

live earth-life as you live it, passionately
working the stubborn grain of what is true.

Violence and passion cast their imagery:
then, in a mind that's strong enough to view

their rearing shapes with unmoved certainty
the moon shines down and moulds those forms anew

to antithetical images, all set free
from sweat and impact. Knowledge splits in two:

only the wisdom gained impulsively
by saturation in the living brine, as you

have saturated, has the lens to see
her calm, eroded face.
                              All this you knew.

So, silver on your brush, you paint the moon,
anchored in time, untouchable in space,
marked with a faintly-smiling human face
remote, yet pitying our long misfortune.

You know her, for you know her opposite:
earth, where we hold to life with clutch and clang
knowing death waits (by sly cell? or bold bang?)
raising our structures on the mounds of grit.

We use her calm to diagnose our strife.
She borrows from the sun to flood our night,
and, queen of mirrors, gives us our own truth.

They yearn to drill her like a hollow tooth:
but you, on your bare hills, receive her light,
and gather moondust as art gathers life.

Green Fingers

*to Elizabeth Jennings
in Oxford*

THE intricate city suspended above fire.
A pavement of logic strung on cables of faith.
Belief in the known fire and the unknown fire.
A programme for eternity rooted in time.
Expectations built stone by stone, like the square
towers seen from the river bank. Cool water,
cool stone. And underneath, the fire.

And the fire also is an intricate city.
Cat-walks of the damned, threaded with souls
all humping loads of disappointment. Fire
maddens their veins. Without punishment
would not the city pavements crack and vanish?

Perhaps these fictions are worth it, for the city.
The squared stones of faith, balanced above fire,
are solid under the wind-beaten towers:
and the towers point calmly towards the fiction of heaven.

System, system: that chiming Italian metre,
a threefold music for a threefold theme:
no hope: all hope: effortless fulfilment.

The abstract city of Dante holds also real

fountains that leap in the hot squares of Rome,
the Lambretta's cough in rainy Florence, its walls
flower-hung, picture-hung, throned in Tuscan pride—
no place on earth so solid and so fine.
I know your thought, Elizabeth: you long
to orchestrate a Tuscany of the mind:
as solid and green as those tower-crowned hills,
as native to the green as those white oxen.

                                        Squares,
a pattern of rectangles, a true city
where feet can wander and always find their way:
cafés where lovers or disputants can linger:

you write these things in your book of life, as I do.

Black tarantulas sidle along the cables of faith, which have
become threads of their rubbery bird-murdering webs.

The warm spring mud is full of horse-leeches.

The Pope is a mandril. The Cardinals are mandrils. The
Archbishop's robe hides a narrow, haired baboon-body.
The floor of the confessional box is slippery with fruit-
rinds and stale droppings. All the time the saints absent-
mindedly scratch their rainbow-coloured tumescent nates.

The pavement shivers. Leviathan is trying to batter his
way up from the underground lake.

The upper slopes of the Himalayas seem domestic and
companionable when viewed from the electrically-cooled
vacuum of modern loneliness.

The beautifully-swept boulevards go round in concentric
circles. You could walk and walk for your whole life on
bare clean asphalt, completely unmarked save for, every

few yards, a drop or two of spittle: the drool of the police-dogs. You never see the dogs: they are always round the next curve, and the next curve is always the same as the one behind. Realizing that walking will take you nowhere, you realize also that if you stop walking you will instantly drop through a hole in the pavement and hang on the spider-webs, twitching and waiting.

Suddenly, to your joy and astonishment, the high concrete walls part to reveal a narrow path. You follow it between board fences. A street, an ordinary human street, with children marking out the pavement for hopscotch and a man oiling a bicycle! Are you home at last? In the end house, faces appear at the window; hands beckon. The door opens. Your room is ready. You feel relief and gratitude; but, silently, they point to the cellar steps descending steeply into the darkness.

Down *there?*

The cellar stairs are dark. I hear your tread.
Your fingers trace the cold and sweating wall.
The cellar is a household of the dead.

You never wanted to go down at all:
Whole weeks, whole months, you breathe that airless
    chill!
The stairs are broken. Now and then you fall,

Lie silent, then get up. Whose is the will
That pushes you inside and locks the door?
Or is it mindless? Does the abandoned mill

That swings its arms in the cold wind, know more

Than I what force it is that sends you down?
I fumble with the bolts. They will not draw.

You must stay there, queen of that fungus town
Throned amid nightmares, till the Thing relents,
Opens the door, and with a wondering frown

You climb, and find us here. Between descents,
You live like us: books, walks, the telephone:
All that long patience Oxford represents.

But down there, in a silence hard as bone,
Breathing through those interminable hours,
Sealed from our air and sunshine, cold, alone,

Somehow your magic works. Darkness devours
All love, all laughter drowns in the black slime:
and yet, from that dead floor, you raise up flowers.

When, patiently, up the dark stairs you climb,
Blinking a little in the sharpened day,
You never fail to tell us, *All that time*

In that dark place, I tended these: rich, gay,
Abundant, there they shine: you hold them out
As modestly as tea-things on a tray.

Green-fingered artist, I see you never doubt
Even in those lost days, denying, stark,
What is the work that you must be about:

A world of colour blossoming in the dark!
Hidden from anguish and the body's fears
Like trustful cattle in the wallowing ark,

Its seeds couch in a soil kept moist for years:

They grow towards your memory of the sun:
There must be something potent in those tears

With which you water them, for all that's done
And seen, and thought of, leaves its residue:
Art finishes what action has begun,

But only if its metaphors are true.
I see your colours and I catch my breath,
For joy that once again you have come through.

Your art will save your life, Elizabeth.

Junk Sculptures

for Lee Lubbers
in Omaha

A note on Talus *He is the iron man in Spenser's* Faerie Queen
*(Book V) given to Sir Artegall, who represents justice, by the goddess
Astraea. Talus is a good character in the poem; it seemed natural to
Spenser to make a robot the servant of justice. We, who have more
experience of robots and slave-machines generally, need not be
so confident. We also remember that Astraea, when the golden age
of humanity ended, withdrew to heaven and was placed among the
stars, under the name of Virgo.*

1

Patiently, your hands moving among the wounds,
you start from a pity that grows,
under a black sky, towards the sun.

On the cold concrete floor your feet pace gently,
back and forth, strong with patience,
whether the earth shakes with the tread of Talus,
or whether the earth, for a little while, is still.

Outside, the black sky is indifferent.
Virgo shines in her appointed remoteness,
cold, in a firmament of endings.

Gently,

among the stalks and shards your hands have rescued,
you move against endings:
you move against the finality of death,
even the death of these gauche remainders.

Junk. Once the poor finery of demented factories.
Now, so soon, blistered with rust, thrown out,
forgotten. Come, laugh your heads off!
The factory's dialect dies into this silence,
this patter of rain on unpatrolled heaps.

No, artificer,

Yours is the wisdom.
Our notions of history are paltry.

What life really ends?

2

To the bonfire, old lexicons. The language of ruins
has altered. Soft rain washes into silence
the message chiselled on stone, and also
dissolves the nail-clippings of Talus. Time
is air, time is rain, weather is *temps*:
temps: temps: the beat of the drumskin.
The old ruin-language is drowned, the syllables
of permanent reproach and warning, *You shall be
as I am*, yet the threat itself bestows a dignity:
*You, even fretful you, have sufficient importance
to become a ruin.* To inspire slow thoughts
of the bitter siege of time, of monuments.

What now?

As every hour the trucks roll up

coming from nowhere and going back to nowhere,
but every hour dumping new loads of junk—

old teeth and hair of Talus! New ruins!
What language now? What runic gibberish?
What can we read in this new cuneiform?

We read the history of Talus and his exile.
Talus, once the servant of justice, has run mad.
When the goddess left him, he forgot his service.
All he remembers is his iron flail.

The inscription tells of Talus seeking forgetfulness,
dying and laughing aloud at his own death
finding his life's nerve in the quickness of death.

The centaurs with their broken hoofs are quiet.
No sound comes to them on the wind.
                                        But you,
on the cold concrete floor, you pause and bend.

3

Your eye, cool astronaut, perceives
relationships.
                    In the cold light
metal, stunned by neglect into a trance
of hopelessness, shams dead.
But not to you. Not to your generous eye,
which moves as an eagle might move among clouds:
thoughtfully, those swollen rain-bearers
gently containing his fragile desires.

Outside, Talus thumps the earth.
In the factories the night-shift has begun,
on the other side of the world it is the day-shift,
but in any case shift, shift, shift, as tired men
minister to the gabbling machines.
                    Talus, Talus is king!

In the banks the computers think about money,
super-highways girdle the earth, leading nowhere:
the bombers stream down the runways. Talus with his
    flail
delights in wreckage.

(*And brusht, and battred them without remorse,*
That on the ground he left full many a corse;
Ne any able was him to withstand,
But he them overthrew both man and horse.)

Yes, man and horse overthrown,
the rider with the ridden, merged at last
in the sadness of defeat.
To the grey asbestos stable built by Talus
defeated centaurs hobble on broken hooves.

Talus watches. He rules.
The centaurs shamble to his feeding troughs.
Galled, melancholy, they are resigned
to half-life. But he, Talus,
rejoices in the wholeness of unceasing death.

He finds his life's nerve in the quickness of death.
The junk-yards are his whispering catacombs.

Talus
child of rape
knowing his queen withdrawn

knowing his queen uplifted
beyond the moon's cold horns
Virgo
        her gaze withdrawn

child of rape

Talus in solitude
clutching his iron flail

thirsty, as we are
for love's metamorphic touch
for change, for life new shaped
with every new-lit dawn

abandoned by his queen
his trusted one
Virgo, her gaze withdrawn

he longs now for death
love's substitute
that other metamorphosis
in death at least to change
to sink into the earth

forgetful mother, whose
rich veins he still remembers
to sink, to find again
her veins, and heat, and change.

When Astraea rose
climbed the unreachable sky
to glitter out of reach
for ever out of reach
and with no downward glance
did Talus long to weep?
His iron eyes are dry.

He lay down in the dust:
then rose, and followed death.

4

But you, Hephaestos on the concrete floor,
move in the freedom of art: the key
to all dimensions lies in your careful hand,
and gently, as a man might move among clouds,
you move against endings.
                                    The broken toys of Talus,
limbs snapped by his appetite for disaster, coils
untwisted, garish carapaces
stripped of their framework, everything uncovered,
ashamed, denuded of purpose, thrown to the rain,
you gather, now, and contemplate.

Folded in secrecy this metal slept
aeons in silent grains, earth's counsel kept.

The drills and crushers came. Rock screamed and broke.
Under a blinding sky the metal woke.

Naked, unshelled: abstracted from the earth:
squeezed through the portals of a second birth.

Melted in unimaginable heat.
All memory burnt away. Then cold, complete,

free from the taint of life, it stands alone.
No need of dialogue with blood and bone.

But time defeats. Rust-blistered chrome subsides
in dumps like the mass graves of suicides.

And there it waits. Till the compassionate eye
weds shape to shape: gives form, gives dignity:

Skilled hands construct what the skilled heart has viewed,
and give not merely life, but plenitude.

These fragments he has loved into wholeness, serve
the single ambition of the black-coated artist:
they testify, they move against endings,
they ask the question: 'What life really ends?'

Watch the rescuing artificer. Deftly
with rubber gloves, he wires their circuits.
In the cold coils of their brains, already they hear
temps, temps, temps. They are coming back into time.

Look up, centaurs! The show is beginning!

He throws a switch.
                They churn, his mannikins,
and roar, flash signals from their eager sockets;
their guts rumble with the digestion of pure energy.

Not the energy of oblivion-seeking Talus, but of life:
the life that once flowed in the limbs of the centaurs,
the life that burns in the prayer of the black-coated man
who watches over life and prays for it not to be spilt,
who moves against endings, against the flail of Talus,
and against the sad captivity of the centaurs.

Lee Lubbers, you showed me this, on the cold concrete
under the school, with the dustbins outside the door,
and beyond the dustbins the black rain and the earth's
    curve.
I was silent, for I was watching a resurrection,
The love of life defeating the lust for death,
A green miracle under the needles of rain.

Artist and priest, I think I understand.
I think I see for a moment with your eyes:
that look upon the earth and see obstinacy,
the obstinacy of man confronting the obstinacy of stone,
of grit, of pebbles and of the furthest stars,
the obstinacy of Talus plotting his own death,
the ugly stubbornness of self-will and waste:

why, these machines are your prayers! I see it all!
your messages beamed to the sharp towers of heaven,
and bouncing back from that Telstar to the balancing
city of man: *Today if ye will hear
my voice, harden not your hearts.* The juke-box mouths
of your harsh toys clack a new idiom
for truths that must continually be said:
for truths that came spilling from the stiff jaws of those
cold agonized bodies that Villon dreamed hanging: stiff
and gibbeted, with the more emphasis praying
*freres humains qui apres nous vivez
n'ayez les cuers contre nous endurcis.*

Those gibbet-stretched culprits resembled human forms
as your loud dolls do: pathetic as caricatures
they state their necessary claim on our compassion.
The allowing of this claim is your life and art:
the bead you draw on the towers of heaven:
and this makes you, a learned man, a priest,
set apart by discipline and sacrifice,
a force of nature also—for nature
re-cycles waste, makes life from husk and dung.

And for this wisdom and this gentleness
my thanks to you, Lee, and your harlequins.

Ferns

for Anthony Conran
in Bangor

YOURS is the steep house on the steep hill.
Below, the hospital. Above, the college.
The town clings to the land's short shoulders.

You chose this place to meet your need for contrast.
Everything here pirouettes with its opposite
in a dance whose music your inner ear
holds cupped.
                    Those ancient hard heads,
the clustered mountains, some of earth's oldest rocks,
light green or purple, grass, stone or heather,
changing with the light that walks among the clouds,
above the heavy layers of the sea
(unalterably of its own way of thinking,
dismantling and building, eating and disgorging,
cold and sensual with its own salt
and its own secrets):
                    two grandeurs
to orchestrate with the ordinariness of the streets,
the commonplaces of shop-front and semi,
the leaded panes in the boarding-house front porch.
Now *there*'s a challenge for a true artist,
such as God, or one of his poor worshippers!

In Caernarvonshire. Gull-scream and cloud-drift.
On this long shelf, 'the stone's
in the midst of all' most literally.
The thin soil lies a few inches deep
spreadeagled over rock, strained through by rain.
Everywhere, boulders and outcroppings
prod grey through green. In valleys near the sky
the abandoned quarries sigh to the deaf wind:
thousands of tons of slate beneath your hand,
level green tracks where little railways climbed,
and higher up, shale. Scree. The Elephant's
long corrugated trunk, his patient head.

Nothing can live here that does not love stone.

Water among the rocks. The dark
drip into a stone cup. Perfection,
the natural chiselled goblet. But of a chillness
inviting nothing from the onlooker.
The water hurries as if to escape a plague,
keeping its cold integrity. It runs
and leaps down the unsunned cleft. The mountain
listens.
          And the fern holds on,
rooted in any cranny, green and curling,
its form a patient embroidery, a scroll,
one of a set of variations on
a shape basically as simple as an egg
and full of possibilities as a hand:
it grows, it climbs, it unfolds,
not to be questioned, permanently there,
younger than nothing but the rocks and water.

Or in the town. The steps behind your house.
Handrail and blackened brick. The fern is there
sprouting from crevices, ignoring our

broken-winded voices as we drag
ourselves up to the road that leads to the college.

They clench and curl towards the rainy sky.
And out in your back yard, in grey stone troughs,
are some you tend:
                    you garner, name, and love.

They come to my aid, Tony, your green friends:
your house-mates in their troughs of mould outside
your kitchen window: yes, they help me.
They bring me calming thoughts: like hard brooms
they sweep the hot pavement of my life
cleansing its dry surface like a cool green wind.
This is because they speak to me of beginnings,
and of the time before the beginnings:
millions of years of water, stone, and cloud.

Oh, it helps, on the hot pavement,
so crowded with bumping bodies, so littered,
rank with the sweat of toil and the sweat of fear,
it helps to be guided by those stubborn tendrils,
those unambiguous wavings of semaphore
from the other end of the ravine of time:
it helps, amid the jostling of impulses,
the snatching for scraps of love and shreds of pleasure,
amid the suction of lips, the slop and wallow
of digestion, the throbbing mast of lust,
it steadies me to think of the beginnings,
and of the time before the beginnings,

WHEN

life had not yet arrived

the vapour rising upward from the hot ball of earth had

condensed into thick clouds which continually let fall their rain, hissing on to bare rocks too hot for the hand (but there were no hands) and then gathering into steamy pools and then into lakes and then into the planet-girdling oceans, but such oceans! so clean and empty, thousands of miles of water without one speck of seaweed, not the smallest jellyfish, no hungry, exploring crumb of life, only the plashing and tumbling of the water and the drifting of thick white cloud, and the beat of rain on the rocks: no cry of voice, no thought, no desire, except perhaps the desire of earth itself, deep in those veins of fire, the longing to be swarmed over, to be trampled, populated, used:

AND WHEN

fear had not yet arrived

because of course there must have been movement, rattle and slide of loosened stone, even thunder of surf there must have been: surely there were storms, wind must have hastened from one point of the compass to another (but there was no compass, nor mind to reckon its degrees), wind must have shoved at the rocks, piled up the waves: there were certainly volcanoes, sudden unmannerly lava-belchings with smoke and fire, and who doubts that there were tornadoes, twisting up columns of water, sending the great pillars walking onward with idle, swaying menace: idle because no one feared being sucked up or smashed, there was no drowning, no burying, no overwhelming, no shrieking for pity, no rattling the last desperate breath into the terrified lung: there was movement, there was collision, there was destruction, but there was no fear:

AND WHEN

love, equally, had not yet arrived

there was nowhere on the earth one single cluster of
organized matter which perceived another cluster of
matter organized in what was basically the same way, yet
with certain all-important and delicious differences, and
sent flashing like an electric hare round the circuit of its
nervous impulses the message: Happiness would be to
own *that*.

And all this nothingness took place in secret!
The clouds made a thick white curtain, translucent
but concealing, to ward off the brooding sun.

It must have been like an enormous bathroom.
So clean, so void of event: it rests me
to think of it, Tony!
                    Tugged every way by life,
when there seems too damned much of everything,
and I have fears that I may not cease to be,
but live on through storm's cycle and epicycle,
through aeons of devouring and of being devoured,
I like to think of those millions of years of nothing.

Of course, sooner or later the action had to start.
God, or whatever, would never have allowed it
to hang back for always.
                    So the hot gases, or something,
acted on by something, perhaps the strong sunlight,
began to form these complicated patterns
of chemical reaction, or something:
and after a lot of nobody-quite-knows-what,
something happened that we do not understand,
but we see it has an affinity with ourselves
and we call it 'life'.
                    Yes, 'life' began, that grand

solemn fever of which all of us are dying,
and even God has forgotten how to cure!

The shoots you cherish curl upwards from the stone.
They embody every kind of patience,
including that of your poems. The green they show
is earth's basic livery. Unconcerned at weather
that would lash back more opportunist flowers,
they acknowledge no environment as master.

Their one colour is stronger than the hue of flowers.
Basically simple in structure, their patience
gives them the holy power to astonish: they show
intricate lace-patterns, raising from cracks in the stone
delicate opening fingers to caress the weather.
This is why you love them, undiscourageable master,

intent on your page of cool petal and stone,
assembling grain by grain in the dispersing weather
a soil firm enough for your unsentimental flowers:
enamelled, regal, giving to life their master
the strong homage of art, which cannot show
love except where love is. Their glowing patience

mellows the air of your steep house, that stone
ledge where you perch above your century's weather
still as a hawk, waiting for movement to show
far down among the trembling grass and flowers,
no less potent than that fierce bird to master
your fluttering hunger with the hunter's patience,

yet unlike him in what your gestures show.
Life, not death, signals from your high stone:
the wish to tend and nourish, not the impatience
to scatter blood amid the scent of flowers:
not the suddenness of the chill and troubled weather
but the slow stubborn love of the art you master.

Poet, guard your love. Feed your rooted patience.
Only such as you will have any good to show
for these blank, scurrying years. The time of the stone
is on us now, the life-denying weather
of dust-storm and mistral. Withstand it, master,
and may your dreams be garlands of cool flowers.

How this time's dead weather bruises our living patience.
Thank God, in this place of stone, one knot of flowers:
Amid the bawling freak-show one quiet master!

Take the wind, poem, in your pregnant sails.
Turn our head towards less shallow waters.
He whom we praise is a poet, not a plant.
And yet:
my mind comes back to Ovid and his changes.
Sitting in Eirian's cottage above the sea,
I have no copy of *Metamorphoses* here,
but your own sheaf of poems of that name
gives me the images I want:
                              the rain is 'the time
of crossed circles', a girl's sleep floats downstream
in the guise of drowned Ophelia, also a swan
arching its lute-neck.
                        Ovid would have relished
your poems for their strong juxtapositions:
painting the country of your feelings as
'the strange land humped like a weasel's back
where bedouin ride'.
                      Tony, you take your risks
and root yourself high up on the cliff-face.

It is his suddenness you learn from,
that Roman, strong-willed, in his graver years
his imagination no longer like a furry bunny
hopping amid tangles, diving to a burrow,

but like an unexpected kangaroo
as yet undreamt of, leaping the steady walls
of Rome. His not-yet-exiled eyes
saw shape as motion.
                    And all true poets have
seen with the eyes of Naso, when the weight
of the month grows lighter, and sharp moon
grins down: then their tides pull like a woman's,
and Ovid's liquefaction flows to theirs.
'Daphne with her thighs in bark
Stretches towards me leafy hands':
This sight was vouched for in London, W.8:
the victor's leaf, the girl's blood yielding to sap
(much the same colour when enclosed in veins)!

So Ovid gives me the answer, in the end.
The hard spores of your art unfold to ferns:
the cool heraldic fronds, the ancient strength:
pain, love and knowledge rooted among the rocks.

And there is courage here, friend, for such as we,
making our music in a tone-deaf world.
The ferns grow green with or without approval.
They spread their fans whether they are seen or not.
There is much virtue in these ancient leaves.

THE ARTISTS

BILL COLEMAN, jazz trumpeter, born in Paris, Kentucky, has lived most of his mature life in Paris, France, where he made famous recordings in the thirties with Django Reinhardt; he spent the war years back in America, playing and recording with Teddy Wilson, John Kirby, Coleman Hawkins, Benny Carter, etc.; returned to Paris in 1948, and has stayed there ever since dominating the French jazz scene.

VICTOR NEEP, English artist (of partly Hebridean stock), lives and works in North Wales; his paintings and metal constructions are widely on view, particularly in the north of England.

ELIZABETH JENNINGS, English poet, lives in Oxford; no trouble or difficulty has ever stopped her working; *Collected Poems*, 1967; volume out since.

LEE LUBBERS, S.J., is Chairman of the Fine Arts Department of Creighton University, Omaha, Nebraska, and a practising artist mainly interested in 'junk sculpture'.

ANTHONY CONRAN, English poet with Welsh and Irish blood, lives in the Victor Neep belt of North Wales; many publications; *Collected Poems* 1966, *Penguin Book of Welsh Verse* 1967.